365 Days of Spirituality and Mindfulness

A Quote  Peace

By Victoria Adelar

Victoria Adelar has asserted her moral right to be identified as the author of this work in accordance with the Copyright, Designs and Patents Act 1988.

All rights reserved. No part of this publication may be produced, stored in a retrieval system, or transmitted in any form or by any means, electronic, mechanical, photocopying or otherwise without the prior permission of the copyright owner.

Introduction

The following 365 quotes, across 12 mindful themes, are taken from people from many walks of life to help give perspective and clear your mind.

Please pick up and put down the book as you see fit, contemplating and meditating on the words and themes written down.

I hope this brings you joy and inner space and inspires you to build a better world.

Table of Contents

CHAPTER 1: GRATITUDE 5

CHAPTER 2: GIVING 11

CHAPTER 3: PRESENCE 16

CHAPTER 4: PEACE 21

CHAPTER 5: PATIENCE 26

CHAPTER 6: ACCEPTANCE 32

CHAPTER 7: FORGIVENESS 37

CHAPTER 8: ABUNDANCE 43

CHAPTER 9: SELF LOVE 49

CHAPTER 10: FEAR AND ANXIETY 55

CHAPTER 11: CREATIVITY 61

CHAPTER 12: BREATHING, NATURE AND THE UNIVERSE 67

Chapter 1: Gratitude

The essence of all beautiful art, all great art, is gratitude.
Friedrich Nietzsche 1844-1900

When I started counting my blessings, my whole life turned around.
Willie Nelson 1933-

Piglet noticed that even though he had a very small heart, it could hold a rather large amount of Gratitude.
A.A. Milne 1882-1956

This a wonderful day. I've never seen this one before.
Maya Angelou 1928-2014

Enough is a feast.
Buddhist proverb

Acknowledging the good that you already have in your life is the foundation for all abundance.
Eckhart Tolle 1948-

My day begins and ends with gratitude.
Louise Hay 1926-2017

There are only two ways to live your life. One is as though nothing is a miracle. The other is as though everything is a miracle.
Albert Einstein 1879-1955

Enjoy the little things, for one day you may look back and realize they were the big things.
Robert Brault 1963-

If the only prayer you said in your whole life was, thank you, that would suffice.
Meister Eckhart 1260-1328

Be thankful for what you have; you'll end up having more. If you concentrate on what you don't have, you will never, ever have enough.
Oprah Winfrey 1954-

Some people grumble that roses have thorns; I am grateful that thorns have roses.
Jean-Baptiste Alphonse Karr 1808-1890

Happiness cannot be travelled to, owned, earned, worn or consumed. Happiness is the spiritual experience of living every minute with love, grace, and gratitude.
Denis Waitley 1933-

Gratitude is riches. Complaint is poverty.
Doris Day 1922-2019

Gratitude is not only the greatest of virtues, but the parent of all others.
Marcus Tullius Cicero 106 BC - 43 BC

When I count my blessings, I find you in every one.
Richelle E. Goodrich 1968-

Count your summers, not your winters.
Matshona Dhliwayo

Be thankful that you have clothes to wear, food to eat and a place to sleep.
Lailah Gifty Akita

For one minute, walk outside, stand there, in silence. Look up at the sky and contemplate how amazing life is.
Unknown.

I feel a very unusual sensation - if it is not indigestion, I think it must be gratitude.
Benjamin Disraeli 1804-1881

Every morning, I wake up and think about 10 different things I'm thankful for, and I continue to spread that love throughout the day, always visualizing, meditating, and growing.
Shameik Moore 1995-

I have a lot to be thankful for. I am healthy, happy and I am loved.
Reba McEntire 1955-

It is not joy that makes us grateful, it is gratitude that makes us joyful.
David Steindl-Rast 1926-

Gratitude changes everything.
Anonymous

Be happy for this moment. This moment is your life.
Omar Khayyam 1048-1131

Through the eyes of gratitude, everything is a miracle.
Mary Davis 1954-

Gratitude unlocks the fullness of life. It turns what we have into enough, and more. It turns denial into acceptance, chaos to order, confusion to clarity. It can turn a meal into a feast, a house into a home, a stranger into a friend. Gratitude makes sense of our past, brings peace for today and creates a vision for tomorrow.
Melody Beattie 1948-

Just tell yourself, Duckie, you're really quite lucky.
Dr. Seuss 1904-1991

I'd like to live as a poor man with lots of money.
Pablo Picasso 1881-1973

Yesterday's the past, tomorrow's the future, but today is a gift. That's why it's called the present.
Bill Keane 1922-2011

If you are really thankful, what do you do? You share.
W. Clement Stone 1902-2002

Chapter 2: Giving

We make a living by what we get, but we make a life by what we give.
Winston Churchill 1874-1965

No one is useless in this world who lightens the burdens of another.
Charles Dickens 1812-1870

Those who are happiest are those who do the most for others.
Booker T. Washington 1856-1915

Give, and it will be given to you. A good measure, pressed down, shaken together and running over, will be poured into your lap. For with the measure you use, it will be measured to you.
Luke 6:38

Love only grows by sharing. You can only have more for yourself by giving it away to others.
Brian Tracy 1975-

If we have no peace, it is because we have forgotten that we belong to each other.
Mother Teresa 1910-1997

No one has ever become poor by giving.
Anne Frank 1929-1945

Your successes and happiness are forgiven you only if you generously consent to share them.
Albert Camus 1913-1960

I must be willing to give whatever it takes to do good to others. This requires that I be willing to give until it hurts. Otherwise, there is no true love in me, and I bring injustice, not peace, to those around me.
Mother Teresa 1910-1997

See the light in others and treat them as if that is all you see.
Wayne Dyer 1940-2015

In our willingness to give that which we seek, we keep the abundance of the universe circulating in our lives.
Deepak Chopra 1946-

Wars are never fought for altruistic reasons.
Arundhati Roy 1961-

You can give without loving, but you cannot love without giving.
Amy Carmichael 1867-1951

For pleasure has no relish unless we share it.
Virginia Woolf 1882-1941

For it is in giving that we receive.
Francis of Assisi 1182 - 1226

Our prime purpose in this life is to help others. And if you can't help them, at least don't hurt them.
Dalai Lama 1935-

If you have a candle, the light won't glow any dimmer if I light yours off mine.
Steven Tyler 1948-

Everybody wants to save the Earth; nobody wants to help Mom do the dishes.
P. J. O'Rourke 1947-

Practice kindness all day to everybody and you will realize you're already in heaven now.
Jack Kerouac 1922-1969

We only have what we give.
Isabel Allende 1942-

If you're in the luckiest one percent of humanity, you owe it to the rest of humanity to think about the other 99 percent.
Warren Buffett 1930-

The best way to find yourself is to lose yourself in the service of others.
Mahatma Gandhi 1869-1948

When you stop living for luxuries you understand the real meaning of life.
Abdul Sattar Edhi 1928-2016

One of the most important things you can do on this earth is to let people know they are not alone.
Shannon L. Alder

Remember this. Hold on to this. This is the only perfection there is, the perfection of helping others. This is the only thing we can do that has any lasting meaning. This is why we're here. To make each other feel safe.
Andre Agassi 1970-

Giving opens the way for receiving.
Florence Scovel Shinn 1871-1940

Kindness in words creates confidence. Kindness in thinking creates profoundness. Kindness in giving creates love.
Lao Tzu

If you have much, give of your wealth; If you have little, give of your heart.
Arab proverb

Chapter 3: Presence

Yesterday is gone. Tomorrow has not yet come. We have only today. Let us begin.
Mother Theresa 1910-1997

To a mind that is still the whole universe surrenders.
Lao Tzu

When adversity strikes, that's when you have to be the most calm. Take a step back, stay strong, stay grounded and press on.
LL Cool J 1968-

Let others see their own greatness when looking in your eyes.
Mollie Marti

Be here now.
Ram Dass 1931-

Forever is composed of nows.
Emily Dickinson 1830-1886

Life is a journey, not a destination.
Ralph Waldo Emerson 1803-1882

If you want to conquer the anxiety of life, live in the moment, live in the breath.
Amit Ray 1960-

Today is yours to shape. Create a masterpiece!
Steve Maraboli 1975-

Mindfulness isn't difficult, we just need to remember to do it.
Sharon Salzberg 1952-

All that is important is this one moment in movement. Make the moment important, vital, and worth living. Do not let it slip away unnoticed and unused.
Martha Graham 1894-1991

Real generosity towards the future lies in giving all to the present.
Albert Camus 1913-1960

The best and most beautiful things in the world cannot be seen or even touched. They must be felt with the heart.
Helen Keller 1880-1968

I have realized that the past and future are real illusions, that they exist in the present, which is what there is and all there is.
Alan Watts 1915-1973

The best way out is always through.
Robert Frost 1874-1963

When you are here and now, sitting totally, not jumping ahead, the miracle has happened. To be in the moment is the miracle.
Osho 1931-1990

Don't let procrastination take over your life. Be brave and take risks. Your life is happening right now.
Roy T. Bennett 1939-2014

In the presence of eternity, the mountains are as transient as the clouds.
Robert G. Ingersoll 1833-1899

Time is an illusion.
Albert Einstein 1879-1955

The truth is that you already are what you are seeking.
Adyashanti 1962-

Realize deeply that the present moment is all you have. Make the now the primary focus of your life.
Eckhart Tolle 1948-

All that moves exhausts itself eventually. Only that which is still is for always.
Sadhguru Jaggi Vasudev 1957-

Everything has beauty, but not everyone sees it.
Confucius 551 BC-479 BC

At some point you just have to let go of what you thought should happen and live in what is happening.
Anonymous

Yesterday is history. Tomorrow is a mystery. Today is a gift. That is why it is called the present.
Alice Morse Earle 1851-1911

Intelligence is the capacity to be reborn again and again. To die to the past is intelligence, and to live in the present is intelligence.
Osho 1931-1990

In the beginner's mind there are many possibilities, but in the expert's there are few.
Shunryu Suzuki 1904-1971

Let go or be dragged.
Zen Proverb

I have lived with several Zen masters - all of them cats.
Eckhart Tolle 1948-

Do not seek the truth, only cease to cherish your opinions.
Seng-ts'an 529-606

Beneath your words is written the Word of God.
A Course in Miracles

Chapter 4: Peace

It isn't enough to talk about peace. One must believe in it. And it isn't enough to believe in it. One must work at it.
Eleanor Roosevelt 1884-1962

War is never a lasting solution for any problem.
A. P. J. Abdul Kalam 1931-2015

If you cannot find peace within yourself, you will never find it anywhere else.
Marvin Gaye 1939-1984

Happiness is when what you think, what you say, and what you do are in harmony.
Mahatma Gandhi 1869-1948

If it costs your inner peace, it is too expensive.
Anonymous

We are all different. Don't judge, understand instead.
Roy T. Bennett 1939-2014

Peace is always beautiful.
Walt Whitman 1819-1892

One love, one heart, one destiny.
Bob Marley 1945-1981

Success isn't measured by money or power or social rank. Success is measured by your discipline and inner peace.
Mike Ditka 1939-

Do not feel lonely. The entire universe is inside of you.
Rumi 1207-1273

Happiness. Contentment. Inner peace. Have you ever gone looking for something, only to realize you had it with you the whole time?
Anonymous

Virtue is harmony.
Pythagoras

The best fighter is never angry.
Lao Tzu

Ego says - Once everything falls into place, I'll feel inner peace. Spirit says – Find your inner peace and then everything will fall into place.
Marianne Williamson 1952-

In the madness, you have to find calm.
Lupita Nyong'o 1983-

Folks are usually about as happy as they make their minds up to be.
Abraham Lincoln 1809-1865

Peace begins with a smile.
Mother Teresa 1910-1997

Surrender to what is, let go of what was, have faith in what will be.
Sonia Ricotti 1965-

Do not let the behaviour of others destroy your inner peace.
Dalai Lama 1935-

Count your age by friends, not years. Count your life by smiles, not tears.
John Lennon 1940-1980

Peace is not absence of conflict, it is the ability to handle conflict by peaceful means.
Ronald Reagan 1911-2004

The body is your temple. Keep it pure and clean for the soul to reside in.
B.K.S. Iyengar 1918-2014

We are all on a journey to mastering our inner peace.
Raheem DeVaughn 1975-

There is always room for change, but you have to be open to that change.
Kathryn Budig 1982-

We don't realize that, somewhere within us all, there does exist a supreme self who is eternally at peace.
Elizabeth Gilbert 1969-

Don't cry because it's over, smile because it happened.
Dr. Seuss 1904-1991

I meditate so I know how to find a peaceful place within to be calm and peaceful.
Roseanne Barr 1952-

Inner peace is our natural state.
Anonymous

Sleep is God. Go worship.
Jim Butcher 1971-

An eye for an eye will only make the whole world blind.
Mahatma Gandhi 1869-1948

Chapter 5: Patience

Patience is a virtue.
Proverb

Good things come to those who wait.
Proverb

Infinite patience produces immediate results.
Foundation for Inner Peace, A Course in Miracles

Life was always a matter of waiting for the right moment to act.
Paulo Coelho 1947-

Patience is bitter, but its fruit is sweet.
Aristotle 384 BC - 322 BC

Nothing good ever comes out of hurry and frustration, only misery.
Auliq Ice

The key to everything is patience. You get the chicken by hatching the egg, not by smashing it.
Arnold H. Glasgow 1905-1998

Be worthy, love, and love will come.
Louisa May Alcott 1832-1888

The strongest of all warriors are these two - Time and Patience.
Leo Tolstoy 1828-1910

She was always waiting, it seemed to be her forte.
D.H. Lawrence 1885-1930

It is very strange that the years teach us patience - that the shorter our time, the greater our capacity for waiting.
Elizabeth Taylor 1932-2011

The time you feel lonely is the time you most need to be by yourself.
Douglas Coupland 1961-

Having perfected our disguise, we spend our lives searching for someone we don't fool.
Robert Brault 1963-

When anger rises, think of the consequences.
Confucius 551 BC-479 BC

Some people can never understand that you have to wait, even for the best of things, until the right time comes.
Franklin D. Roosevelt 1882-1945

I have no plan. I will leave it to the good things and good times to find me.
Nimrat Kaur 1982-

An alternative to love is not hate but patience.
Santosh Kalwar 1982-

Nature does not hurry, yet everything is accomplished.
Lao Tzu

Rushing, rushing, rushing. We are always rushing.
Cecelia Ahern 1981-

If you are irritated by every rub, how will your mirror be polished?
Rumi 1207-1273

It will happen but it will take time.
John Bowlby 1907-1990

Wisely and slow; they stumble that run fast.
William Shakespeare 1564-1616

Patience is not passive, on the contrary, it is concentrated strength.
Bruce Lee 1940-1973

The hurrier I go, the behinder I get.
Lewis Carroll 1832-1898

Impatience can cause wise people to do foolish things.
Janette Oke 1935-

Are you aware that rushing toward a goal is a sublimated deathwish? It's no coincidence we call them 'deadlines'.
Tom Robbins 1932-

Man hurries, God does not. That is why man's works are uncertain and maimed, while God's are flawless and sure. My eyes welling with tears, I vowed never to transgress this eternal law again. Like a tree I would be blasted by wind, struck by sun and rain, and would wait with confidence; the long-desired hour of flowering and fruit would come.
Nikos Kazantzakis 1883-1957

Don't rush into love. You'll find the person meant for you when you least expect it.
Franzie Gubatina

Adopt the pace of nature: her secret is patience.
Ralph Waldo Emerson 1803-1882

Actually, I'm an overnight success, but it took twenty years.
Monty Hall 1921-2017

Rome wasn't built in a day.
Proverb

Chapter 6: Acceptance

The greatest gift that you can give to others is the gift of unconditional love and acceptance.
Brian Tracy 1944-

Wanting to be someone else is a waste of the person you are.
Marilyn Monroe 1926-1962

Understanding is the first step to acceptance, and only with acceptance can there be recovery.
J. K. Rowling 1965-

If only. Those must be the two saddest words in the world.
Mercedes Lackey 1950-

When you live in complete acceptance of what is, that is the end of all drama in your life.
Eckhart Tolle 1948-

Life is 10% what happens to you and 90% how you react to it.
Charles R. Swindoll 1934-

I think tolerance and acceptance and love is something that feeds every community.
Lady Gaga 1986-

Love conquers all things; let us too surrender to Love.
Virgil 70 BC - 19 BC

Because one believes in oneself, one doesn't try to convince others. Because one is content with oneself, one doesn't need other's approval. Because one accepts oneself, the whole world accepts him or her.
Lao Tzu

The creative process is a process of surrender, not control.
Julia Cameron 1948-

I never regret anything. Because every little detail of your life is what made you into who you are in the end.
Drew Barrymore 1975-

Change is the only constant in life.
Heraclitus 535 BC – 475 BC

I am dead, but it's not so bad. I've learned to live with it.
Isaac Marion 1981-

Happiness can exist only in acceptance.
George Orwell 1903-1950

The best way to find out if you can trust somebody is to trust them.
Ernest Hemingway 1899-1961

Acceptance of the unacceptable is the greatest source of grace in this world.
Eckhart Tolle 1948-

After a storm comes a calm.
Matthew Henry 1662-1714

You can control two things: your work ethic and your attitude about anything.
Ali Krieger 1984-

Acceptance doesn't mean resignation; it means understanding that something is what it is and that there's got to be a way through it.
Michael J. Fox 1961-

Tension is who you think you should be. Relaxation is who you are.
Chinese Proverb

You could not step twice into the same river.
Heraclitus 535 BC – 475 BC

The more you know who you are, and what you want, the less you let things upset you.
Stephanie Perkins

You can't stop the waves, but you can learn to surf.
Jon Kabat-Zinn 1944-

Acceptance of what has happened is the first step to overcoming the consequences of any misfortune.
William James 1842-1910

Embrace all of life, fall in love, that is how you conquer fear.
Maria Koszler

At fifteen life had taught me undeniably that surrender, in its place, was as honourable as resistance, especially if one had no choice.
Maya Angelou 1928-2014

We must let go of the life we have planned, to accept the one that is waiting for us.
Joseph Campbell 1904 - 1987

I'd rather be hated for who I am, than loved for who I'm not.
Kurt Cobain 1967-1994

You are imperfect, permanently and inevitably flawed. And you are beautiful.
Amy Bloom 1953-

God grant me the serenity to accept the things I cannot change, the courage to change the things I can, and the wisdom to know the difference.
Reinhold Niebuhr 1892-1971

Chapter 7: Forgiveness

To err is human, to forgive, divine.
Alexander Pope 1688-1744

Darkness cannot drive out darkness; only light can do that. Hate cannot drive out hate; only love can do that.
Martin Luther King, Jr. 1929-1968

The only way out of the labyrinth of suffering is to forgive.
John Green 1977-

The highest result of education is tolerance.
Helen Keller 1880-1968

The weak can never forgive. Forgiveness is the attribute of the strong.
Mahatma Gandhi 1869-1948

The wound is the place where the Light enters you.
Rumi 1207-1273

Never judge someone by the way he looks, or a book by the way it's covered; for inside those tattered pages, there's a lot to be discovered.
Stephen Cosgrove 1945-

Men build too many walls and not enough bridges.
Joseph Fort Newton 1876-1950

The heart of a mother is a deep abyss at the bottom of which you will always find forgiveness.
Honore de Balzac 1799 – 1850

The bittersweet about truth is that nothing could be more hurtful, yet nothing could be more helpful.
Mike Norton 1973-

Forgiveness is giving up the hope that the past could have been any different.
Oprah Winfrey 1954-

'I'm sorry about yesterday.' she said. He hung on to his straps and shrugged. 'Yesterday happens.'
Rainbow Rowell 1973-

Forgiveness is not always easy. At times, it feels more painful than the wound we suffered, to forgive the one that inflicted it. And yet, there is no peace without forgiveness.
Marianne Williamson 1952-

Because when there is true equality, resentment does not exist.
Chimamanda Ngozi Adichie 1977-

As smoking is to the lungs, so is resentment to the soul; even one puff is bad for you.
Elizabeth Gilbert 1969-

In the process of letting go you will lose many things from the past, but you will find yourself.
Deepak Chopra 1946-

Life appears to me too short to be spent in nursing animosity or registering wrongs.
Charlotte Bronte 1816-1855

Not forgiving is like drinking rat poison and then waiting for the rat to die.
Anne Lamott 1954-

One thing you can't hide - is when you're crippled inside.
John Lennon 1940-1980

If everyone is moving forward together, then success takes care of itself.
Henry Ford 1863-1947

Six ways to give your mind a break:
1. Stop stressing
2. Stop worrying
3. Give rest to the problems weighing you down
4. Lighten up
5. Forgive yourself
6. Forgive others
Germany Kent 1975-

Remember that when you forgive, you empty yourself so that you may receive.
Debasish Mridha

As above, so below, as within, so without.
Alyson Noel 1965-

Bitterness and unforgiveness block the flow of God's blessing in your life and actually hinder your prayers.
Victoria Osteen 1961-

Forgiveness is a gift you give yourself.
Tony Robbins 1960-

Good judgment comes from experience. Experience comes from bad judgment.
Jim Horning 1942-2013

The most important thing in life is to learn how to give out love, and to let it come in.
Morrie Schwartz 1916-1995

Turn your wounds into wisdom.
Oprah Winfrey 1954-

Pain is inevitable. Suffering is optional.
Buddhist proverb

A happy marriage is the union of two good forgivers.
Ruth Graham 1920-2007

Forgiveness is the key to action and freedom.
Hannah Arendt 1906-1975

Chapter 8: Abundance

Be content with what you have; rejoice in the way things are. When you realize there is nothing lacking, the whole world belongs to you.
Lao Tzu

Abundance is not something we acquire. It is something we tune into.
Wayne Dyer 1940-2015

What is called genius is the abundance of life and health.
Henry David Thoreau 1817-1862

Why are you so enchanted by this world, when a mine of gold lies within you?
Rumi 1207-1273

Abundance is a process of letting go; that which is empty can receive.
Bryant H. McGill 1969-

Having everything is just an expression of complete inner freedom.
Deepak Chopra 1946-

You will receive most when you will expect least.
Santosh Kalwar 1982-

Not what we have but what we enjoy, constitutes our abundance.
Epicurus 341 BC - 270 BC

When you are grateful, fear disappears and abundance appears.
Anthony Robbins 1960-

Gratitude builds a bridge to abundance.
Roy Bennett 1939-2014

Your fortune is not something to find but to unfold.
Eric Butterworth 1916-2003

The key to abundance is meeting limited circumstances with unlimited thoughts.
Marianne Williamson 1952-

True abundance isn't based on our net worth, it's based on our self-worth.
Gabrielle Bernstein 1979-

Abundance arrives in the physical world when the inner world is ready to receive it. When we give ourselves permission to experience abundance, it always shows up.
Pam Malow-Isham

See yourself living in abundance and you will attract it, it always works, it works every time with every person.
Bob Proctor 1934-

Be bold, be brave enough to be your true self.
Queen Latifah 1970-

My Cup Runneth Over.
Psalm 23:5

If you develop an image of success, health, abundance, joy, peace, happiness, nothing on earth will be able to hold those things from you.
Joel Osteen 1963-

Any person who contributes to prosperity must prosper in turn.
Earl Nightingale 1921-1989

Every day is a bank account, and time is our currency. No one is rich, no one is poor, we've got 24 hours each.
Christopher Rice 1978-

There is no scarcity of opportunity to make a living at what you love; there's only scarcity of resolve to make it happen.
Wayne Dyer 1940-2015

Wealth consists not in having great possessions, but in having few wants.
Epictetus 50-135

Remember, no more effort is required to aim high in life, to demand abundance and prosperity than is required to accept misery and poverty.
Napoleon Hill 1883-1970

If you approach the ocean with a cup, you can only take away a cupful; if you approach it with a bucket you can take away a bucketful.
Ramana Maharshi 1879-1950

Freedom's just another word for nothin' left to lose.
Kris Kristofferson 1936-

If you want love and abundance in your life, give it away.
Mark Twain 1835-1910

The universe will reward you for taking risks on its behalf.
Shakti Gawain 1948-2018

Talent is always conscious of its own abundance and does not object to sharing.
Aleksandr Solzhenitsyn 1918-2008

I have the greatest of all riches: that of not desiring them.
Eleonora Duse 1858-1924

If a free society cannot help the many who are poor, it cannot save the few who are rich.
John F. Kennedy 1917-1963

Consider the lilies of the field, how they grow; they toil not, neither do they spin: yet I say unto you, that even Solomon in all his glory was not arrayed like one of these.
Matthew 6:28-30

Chapter 9: Self Love

What lies behind us and what lies before us are tiny matters compared to what lies within us.
Ralph Waldo Emerson 1803-1882

The most terrifying thing is to accept oneself completely.
Carl Jung 1875-1961

If you have the ability to love, love yourself first.
Charles Bukowski 1920-1994

You were born an original work of art. Stay original always. Originals cost more than imitations.
Suzy Kassem 1975-

I am my own experiment. I am my own work of art.
Madonna 1958-

The worst loneliness is to not be comfortable with yourself.
Mark Twain 1835-1910

Love is a flame that burns everything other than itself. It is the destruction of all that is false and the fulfilment of all that is true.
Adyashanti 1962-

Strive not to be a success, but rather to be of value.
Albert Einstein 1879-1955

You have to expect things of yourself before you can do them.
Michael Jordan 1963-

If you knew who walked beside you at all times, on the path that you have chosen, you could never experience fear or doubt again.
Wayne Dyer 1940-2015

Anyone who has a continuous smile on his face conceals a toughness that is almost frightening.
Greta Garbo 1905-1990

Somewhere behind the athlete you've become and the hours of practice and the coaches who have pushed you is a little girl who fell in love with the game and never looked back... play for her.
Mia Hamm 1972-

...If you can trust yourself when all men doubt you, but make allowance for their doubting too...
Rudyard Kipling 1865- 1936

Whether you think you can or think you can't, you are right.
Henry Ford 1863-1947

Through my education, I didn't just develop skills, I didn't just develop the ability to learn, but I developed confidence.
Michelle Obama 1964-

The only way to find true happiness is to risk being completely cut open.
Chuck Palahniuk 1962-

Once you start laughing, you start healing.
Sherry Argov 1977-

To say I love you one must know first how to say the I.
Ayn Rand 1905-1982

Too many people overvalue what they are not and undervalue what they are.
Malcolm S. Forbes 1919-1990

Yesterday I was clever, so I wanted to change the world. Today I am wise, so I am changing myself.
Rumi 1207-1273

The most sophisticated people I know - inside they are all children.
Jim Henson 1936-1990

Happiness is a direction, not a place.
Sydney J. Harris 1917-1986

The better you feel about yourself, the less you feel the need to show off.
Robert Hand 1942-

Love yourself first and everything else falls into line. You really have to love yourself to get anything done in this world.
Lucille Ball 1911-1989

I think the reward for conformity is that everyone likes you except yourself.
Rita Mae Brown 1944-

Amid a world of noisy, shallow actors it is noble to stand aside and say, 'I will simply be'.
Henry David Thoreau 1817-1862

Inaction breeds doubt and fear. Action breeds confidence and courage. If you want to conquer fear, do not sit home and think about it. Go out and get busy.
Dale Carnegie 1888-1955

Act as if what you do makes a difference. It does.
William James 1842-1910

If you hear a voice within you say "you cannot paint," then by all means paint and that voice will be silenced.
Vincent Van Gogh 1853-1890

It is never too late to be what you might have been.
George Eliot 1819-1880

Chapter 10: Fear and Anxiety

Our deepest fear is not that we are inadequate. Our deepest fear is that we are powerful beyond measure. It is our light, not our darkness that most frightens us. We ask ourselves, 'Who am I to be brilliant, gorgeous, talented, fabulous?' Actually, who are you not to be? You are a child of God. Your playing small does not serve the world. There is nothing enlightened about shrinking so that other people won't feel insecure around you. We are all meant to shine, as children do. We were born to make manifest the glory of God that is within us. It's not just in some of us; it's in everyone. And as we let our own light shine, we unconsciously give other people permission to do the same. As we are liberated from our own fear, our presence automatically liberates others.
Marianne Williamson 1952-

Don't believe everything you think. Thoughts are just that - thoughts.
Allan Lokos

Do one thing every day that scares you.
Eleanor Roosevelt 1884-1962

I learned that courage was not the absence of fear, but the triumph over it. The brave man is not he who does not feel afraid, but he who conquers that fear.
Nelson Mandela 1918-2013

Behind every beautiful thing, there's some kind of pain.
Bob Dylan 1941-

Worry never robs tomorrow of its sorrow, it only saps today of its joy.
Leo Buscaglia 1924-1998

You never change your life until you step out of your comfort zone; change begins at the end of your comfort zone.
Roy T. Bennett 1939-2014

Have no fear of perfection - you'll never reach it.
Salvador Dali 1904-1989

You are the sky. Everything else – it's just the weather.
Pema Chödrön 1936-

The storm before the calm.
Cameron Conaway 1985-

It is easier to resist at the beginning than at the end.
Leonardo da Vinci 1452-1519

Man is not worried by real problems so much as by his imagined anxieties about real problems.
Epictetus 55-135

The little things? The little moments? They aren't little.
Jon Kabat-Zinn 1944-

Nothing diminishes anxiety faster than action.
Walter Anderson 1903-1965

Wise is the fool who becomes a master at laughter.
Curtis Tyrone Jones

It's not time to worry yet.
Harper Lee 1926-2016

Times will change for the better when you change.
Maxwell Maltz 1899-1975

You may delay, but time will not.
Benjamin Franklin 1706-1790

Our fatigue is often caused not by work, but by worry, frustration and resentment.
Dale Carnegie 1888-1955

A smooth sea never made a skilled sailor.
Franklin D. Roosevelt 1882-1945

To seek is to suffer. To seek nothing is bliss.
Bodhidharma 483 AD-540 AD

Turn your wounds into wisdom.
Oprah Winfrey 1954-

No pressure, no diamonds.
Thomas Carlyle 1795-1881

Nothing in life is to be feared, it is only to be understood. Now is the time to understand more, so that we may fear less.
Marie Curie 1867-1934

Worry is a misuse of the imagination.
Dan Zadra

Procrastination is the thief of time, collar him.
Charles Dickens 1812-1870

The feeling that any task is a nuisance will soon disappear if it is done in mindfulness.
Thich Nhat Hanh 1926-

Attachment leads to suffering.
Buddha

If you want to test your memory, try to recall what you were worrying about one year ago today.
E. Joseph Cossman 1918-2002

You can't always control what goes on outside. But you can always control what goes on inside.
Wayne Dyer 1940-2015

APPLY WITHIN

You once told me
You wanted to find
Yourself in the world -
And I told you to
First apply within,
To discover the world
within you.

You once told me
You wanted to save
The world from all its wars -
And I told you to
First save yourself
From the world,
And all the wars
You put yourself
Through.

APPLY WITHIN
Suzy Kassem 1975-

Chapter 11: Creativity

The object isn't to make art, it's to be in that wonderful state which makes art inevitable.
Robert Henri 1865-1929

Others have seen what is and asked why. I have seen what could be and asked why not.
Pablo Picasso 1895-1972

It's never too late to have a happy childhood.
Tom Robbins 1932-

Talent hits a target no one else can hit; Genius hits a target no one else can see.
Arthur Schopenhauer 1788-1860

You can never solve a problem on the level on which it was created.
Albert Einstein 1879-1955

You can't use up creativity. The more you use, the more you have.
Maya Angelou 1928-2014

The urge to destroy is also a creative urge.
Mikhail Bakunin 1814-1876

To be creative means to be in love with life. You can be creative only if you love life enough that you want to enhance its beauty, you want to bring a little more music to it, a little more poetry to it, a little more dance to it.
Osho 1931-1990

We do not need magic to transform our world. We carry all of the power we need inside ourselves already.
J. K. Rowling 1965-

Chance favors the prepared mind.
Louis Pasteur 1822-1895

Vulnerability is the birthplace of innovation, creativity and change.
Brene Brown 1965-

There is no time for cut-and-dried monotony. There is time for work. And time for love. That leaves no other time.
Coco Chanel 1883-1971

Creativity is allowing yourself to make mistakes. Art is knowing which ones to keep.
Scott Adams 1957-

The true sign of intelligence is not knowledge but imagination.
Albert Einstein 1879-1955

I like to listen. I have learned a great deal from listening carefully. Most people never listen.
Ernest Hemingway 1899-1961

Mindful and creative, a child who has neither a past, nor examples to follow, nor value judgments, simply lives, speaks and plays in freedom.
Arnaud Desjardins 1925-2011

There are not more than five musical notes, yet the combinations of these five give rise to more melodies than can ever be heard.

There are not more than five primary colours, yet in combination
they produce more hues than can ever been seen.

There are not more than five cardinal tastes, yet combinations of
them yield more flavours than can ever be tasted.
Sun Tzu 545 BC-470 BC

Make it a rule never to give a child a book you would not read yourself.
George Bernard Shaw 1856-1950

Each morning we are born again. What we do today is what matters most.
Buddha

Imitation is suicide.
Ralph Waldo Emerson 1803-1882

Non-judgment quiets the internal dialogue, and this opens once again the doorway to creativity.
Deepak Chopra 1946-

Creativity takes courage.
Henri Matisse 1869-1954

Learn the rules like a pro, so you can break them like an artist.
Pablo Picasso 1895-1972

Beauty will save the world.
Fyodor Dostoyevsky 1821-1881

Having no silence in music is like having no black or white in a painting.
Brian Eno 1948-

The ability to simplify means to eliminate the unnecessary so that the necessary may speak.
Hans Hofmann 1880-1966

Computers are useless. They can only give you answers.
Pablo Picasso 1895-1972

All artists, whether they know it or not create from a place of inner stillness, a place of no mind.
Eckhart Tolle 1948-

There is no genius where there is not simplicity.
Leo Tolstoy 1828-1910

If there's ever a problem, I film it and it's no longer a problem. It's a film.
Andy Warhole 1928-1987

Where the spirit does not work with the hand there is no art.
Leonardo da Vinci 1452-1519

Chapter 12: Breathing, Nature and the Universe

The quality of our breath expresses our inner feelings.
TKV Desikachar 1938-2016

Look deep into nature, and then you will understand everything better.
Albert Einstein 1879-1955

Silence is the language of God, all else is poor translation.
Rumi 1207-1273

When you own your breath, nobody can steal your peace.
Unknown

The nose is for breathing, the mouth is for eating.
Proverb

One of the first conditions of happiness is that the link between Man and Nature shall not be broken.
Leo Tolstoy 1828-1910

The clearest way into the Universe is through a forest wilderness.
John Muir 1838-1914

Breath is the bridge which connects life to consciousness, which unites your body to your thoughts.
Thich Nhat Hanh 1926-

With full attention, you become an instrument of healing on our planet, for all that you touch and every being you meet is then transformed by the power of your focused attention. Therein lies the possibility of Heaven on Earth.
Mary O'Malley 1945-

How foolish to believe we are more powerful than the sea or the sky.
Ruta Sepetys 1967-

If people sat outside and looked at the stars each night, I'll bet they'd live a lot differently.
Bill Watterson 1958-

Earth and sky, woods and fields, lakes and rivers, the mountain and the sea, are excellent schoolmasters, and teach some of us more than we can ever learn from books.
John Lubbock 1834-1913

There is pleasure in the pathless woods, there is rapture in the lonely shore, there is society where none intrudes, by the deep sea, and music in its roar; I love not Man the less, but Nature more.
Lord Byron 1788-1824

Nature never did betray the heart that loved her.
William Wordsworth 1770-1850

Fear is excitement without the breath.
Fritz Perls 1893-1970

You are a child of the universe, no less than the trees and the stars. In the noisy confusion of life, keep peace in your soul.
Max Ehrmann 1872-1945

We know only too well that what we are doing is nothing more than a drop in the ocean. But if the drop were not there, the ocean would be missing something.
Mother Teresa 1910-1997

Earth provides enough to satisfy every man's needs, but not every man's greed.
Mahatma Gandhi 1869-1948

Heaven is under our feet as well as over our heads.
Henry David Thoreau 1817-1862

There is another alphabet, whispering from every leaf, singing from every river, shimmering from every sky.
Dejan Stojanovic 1959-

The breath of life is in the sunlight and the hand of life is in the wind.
Kahlil Gibran 1883-1931

God is silent. Now if only man would shut up.
Woody Allen 1935-

My wish is to stay always like this, living quietly in a corner of nature.
Claude Monet 1840-1926

You are a function of what the whole universe is doing in the same way that a wave is a function of what the whole ocean is doing.
Alan Watts 1915-1973

Weightlessness was wonderful, and I was surprised at how natural it felt.
Ron Garan 1961-

Space is full of wonder. Especially if it's between your ears.
Anthony T. Hincks

One of the basic rules of the universe is that nothing is perfect. Perfection simply doesn't exist.....Without imperfection, neither you nor I would exist
Stephen Hawking 1942-2018

Stillness is the only thing in this world that has no form. But then, it is not really a thing, and it is not of this world.
Eckhart Tolle 1948-

Turn your face to the sun and the shadows fall behind you.
Maori proverb

The mountains are calling, and I must go.
John Muir 1838-1914

Go out tonight and look at the stars. And allow yourself to dream.
Rick Tomlinson 1956-

Finally...

If you enjoyed this book, please feel free to leave a short review on Amazon. I read these reviews personally and any feedback is greatly appreciated.

Many thanks for your support.

Printed in Great Britain
by Amazon